FlashKids
New York

SHERLOCK BONES and the TIMES TABLE ADVENTURE

Illustrated by John Bigwood

Written and edited by Jonny Marx

Designed by Jack Clucas and John Bigwood

Educational Consultancy by Kirstin Swanson

DOCTOR CATSON

SHERLOCK BONES

PROFESSOR MORIRATTY

·SHERLOCK BONES·

My name is Sherlock Bones (world-class detective, professional puzzle solver, and multiplication master). It is my job to solve problems using my superb math skills and to catch cunning criminals when I can.

Can you help me in my Times Table Adventure and track down my evil archenemy, Professor Moriratty, in the process? You will earn medals as you go, and the puzzles will test different times tables as you work your way through the book. My faithful accomplice, Doctor Catson, and I are on board to offer you some helpful hints throughout.

You can use a piece of paper to jot down your work.

The times tables in this book are organized into the following levels:

Pages 3–9: **BRONZE**

2x 5x 10x Tables

Pages 10–17: **SILVER**

3x 4x 8x Tables

Pages 18–25: **GOLD**

6x 7x 9x Tables

Pages 26–31: **PLATINUM**

11x 12x Tables

Page 32: **MIXED MADNESS**

2x to 12x Tables

BRONZE: 2x, 5x, 10x TABLES

Use Sherlock's Secret Solver to see how the **BRONZE** times tables work:

1 x 2 =	1 x 5 =	1 x 10 =
2 x 2 =	2 x 5 =	2 x 10 =
3 x 2 =	3 x 5 =	3 x 10 =
4 x 2 =	4 x 5 =	4 x 10 =
5 x 2 =	5 x 5 =	5 x 10 =
6 x 2 =	6 x 5 =	6 x 10 =
7 x 2 =	7 x 5 =	7 x 10 =
8 x 2 =	8 x 5 =	8 x 10 =
9 x 2 =	9 x 5 =	9 x 10 =
10 x 2 =	10 x 5 =	10 x 10 =
11 x 2 =	11 x 5 =	11 x 10 =
12 x 2 =	12 x 5 =	12 x 10 =

Before you begin, here's my best BRONZE-level tip:

Whenever you multiply an odd number by an even number, the answer will ALWAYS be even. You will only ever end up with an odd answer when you multiply two odd numbers together.

2x TABLES

The 2x table is useful when you want to count pairs of things, such as socks, shoes, gloves, ears, and eyes.

All of the numbers in the 2x table are even, NEVER odd. When a number is in the 2x table it is called a MULTIPLE of 2.

PUZZLE 1

Catson and I are trying to count how many mice are in the kitchen. Luckily, the mice are all dancing in pairs. Can you use your 2x tables to solve the puzzle? Don't forget to use the Secret Solver once you think you have the answer.

There are 6 pairs of dancing mice, so this puzzle can be written as:

$6 \times 2 =$

PUZZLE 2

I asked Catson to check the police station's lost property box for shoes. Can you work out how many shoes she found?

Once you have counted the pairs, the puzzle can be written as:

$\boxed{} \times 2 =$

PUZZLE 3

This one has really confused Catson, but I think I know the answer. Can you solve it, too? You just need to work out how many paw prints have been found at the crime scene.

The puzzle can be written as **eight times two**. What is the answer?

PUZZLE 4

Moving through spaces that contain only **MULTIPLES OF 2,**
can you work out where Catson and I are trying to get to?

The answer is [ ]

QUICKFIRE QUIZ

2 x 2 = [ ]   4 x 2 = [ ]   8 x 2 = [ ]

9 x 2 = [ ]   3 x 2 = [ ]   12 x 2 = [ ]

5 x 2 = [ ]   7 x 2 = [ ]   1 x 2 = [ ]

11 x 2 = [ ]   6 x 2 = [ ]   10 x 2 = [ ]

5x TABLES

The **5x** table is useful when you want to count fingers on each hand and toes on each foot.

Numbers in the 5x table will **ALWAYS** end in a 5 or 0.

PUZZLE 5

Our police badges are pentagonal, meaning they have five sides. How many sides, in total, do the badges below have?

The problem could also be written as: ☐ **x 5 =** ☐

PUZZLE 6

Work out which suspect committed the crime, based on the following clues:

The criminal is **SHORTER** than 12 x 5 centimeters. Therefore, it's not ... ☐

The criminal is **TALLER** than 7 x 5 centimeters. Therefore, it's not ... ☐

The criminal is **NOT** 9 x 5 centimeters tall. Therefore, it's not ... ☐

☐ is the criminal!

60cm · 50cm · 40cm · 30cm · 20cm · 10cm

Alf   Bob   Cassie   Doug

PUZZLE 7

How many days would it take me to solve three cases if they all took five days to crack?

[ ] x 5 = [ ]

PUZZLE 8

I've been busy digging up bones—it's one of my favorite hobbies. There are five bones in each pile. How many bones have I found?

We could also write this problem as:

[ ] x 5 = [ ]

QUICKFIRE QUIZ

4 x 5 = [ ]   9 x 5 = [ ]   2 x 5 = [ ]

11 x 5 = [ ]   12 x 5 = [ ]   5 x 5 = [ ]

8 x 5 = [ ]   3 x 5 = [ ]   10 x 5 = [ ]

1 x 5 = [ ]   6 x 5 = [ ]   7 x 5 = [ ]

10x TABLES

The **10x** table is useful when you want to count fingers on both hands and toes on both feet. The tables in the **BRONZE** section are vital if you're trying to count money. Most currencies use **2**, **5**, and **10** as their denominations or values.

Numbers in the 10x table will ALWAYS end in a 0.

PUZZLE 9

Catson and I have been collecting paw and claw prints as evidence. Each suspect has 10 claws in total. Can you work out the answer?

⬚ x 10 = ⬚

PUZZLE 10

Catson and I get $10 for every case we solve. Look at all of the cases we've solved this week! Can you count them all up and calculate how much we've earned?

⬚ x 10 = $ ⬚

PUZZLE 11

Oh no! Some items have been stolen from Mrs. Moo's shop. Can you solve her times tables to work out how many items, in total, have gone missing?

```
****************************
    3 x 10 apples +
  4 x 10 bottles of milk +
  2 x 10 chocolate bars
--------------------------------
```

TOTAL = ⬚

QUICKFIRE QUIZ

10 x 10 = □   7 x 10 = □   9 x 10 = □

3 x 10 = □   4 x 10 = □   5 x 10 = □

8 x 10 = □   11 x 10 = □   6 x 10 = □

1 x 10 = □   2 x 10 = □   12 x 10 = □

4 = a
5 = b
6 = c
8 = d
10 = e
12 = f
14 = g
15 = h
16 = i
18 = j
20 = k
22 = l
24 = m
25 = n
30 = o
35 = p
40 = q
45 = r
50 = s
55 = t
60 = u
70 = v
80 = w
90 = x
100 = y
110 = z

MORIRATTY MISCHIEF
BRONZE

Something strange is going on. Catson and I found Moriratty's note below at a crime scene. Can you use the key on the left to decode it and to earn your **BRONZE**-level medal?

LET'S SEE HOW GOOD YOU REALLY ARE AT MATH.
I BET YOU CAN'T CRACK MY CLEVER CODE ...

8 x 2 / 2 x 2   12 x 2 / 2 x 2   11 x 5 /
11 x 5   3 x 5   2 x 5 /
6 x 5   1 x 5   10 x 5   5 x 2   9 x 5
7 x 10   2 x 2   11 x 5   3 x 10
9 x 5   10 x 10

CATCH ME IF YOU CAN :)

Moriratty

Moriratty is at the:

□

SILVER: 3x, 4x, 8x TABLES

Use Sherlock's Secret Solver to see how the SILVER times tables work:

1 x 3 =	1 x 4 =	1 x 8 =
2 x 3 =	2 x 4 =	2 x 8 =
3 x 3 =	3 x 4 =	3 x 8 =
4 x 3 =	4 x 4 =	4 x 8 =
5 x 3 =	5 x 4 =	5 x 8 =
6 x 3 =	6 x 4 =	6 x 8 =
7 x 3 =	7 x 4 =	7 x 8 =
8 x 3 =	8 x 4 =	8 x 8 =
9 x 3 =	9 x 4 =	9 x 8 =
10 x 3 =	10 x 4 =	10 x 8 =
11 x 3 =	11 x 4 =	11 x 8 =
12 x 3 =	12 x 4 =	12 x 8 =

Remember, whenever you multiply something by 0, the answer will always be 0. 8 x 0 = 0 and 0 x 8 = 0. NO EXCEPTIONS!

If you're not sure about an answer, you can always try and REVERSE the numbers in the times table. 2 x 8 is the same as 8 x 2, for instance.

3x TABLES

Digits in the **3x** table can be added together to make a multiple of 3. Look at the number 18, for example.

$$18$$
$$1 + 8 = 9$$

9 is a multiple of **3**. Therefore, **18** must be in the **3x** table. Genius! You can try this trick with other numbers even really big ones like . . . **378**

$$3 + 7 + 8 = 18$$
$$1 + 8 = 9$$

378 is in the **3x** table.

PUZZLE 1

Catson has $673 in her bank account. Using the tip on the left, can you work out if this number is in the **3x** table?

$$6 + 7 + 3 = \boxed{}$$

$673 $\boxed{}$ in the **3x** table

I have $2,061 in my bank account. Using the same method, can you work out if this is in the **3x** table?

$$2 + 0 + 6 + 1 = \boxed{}$$

$2,061 $\boxed{}$ in the **3x** table

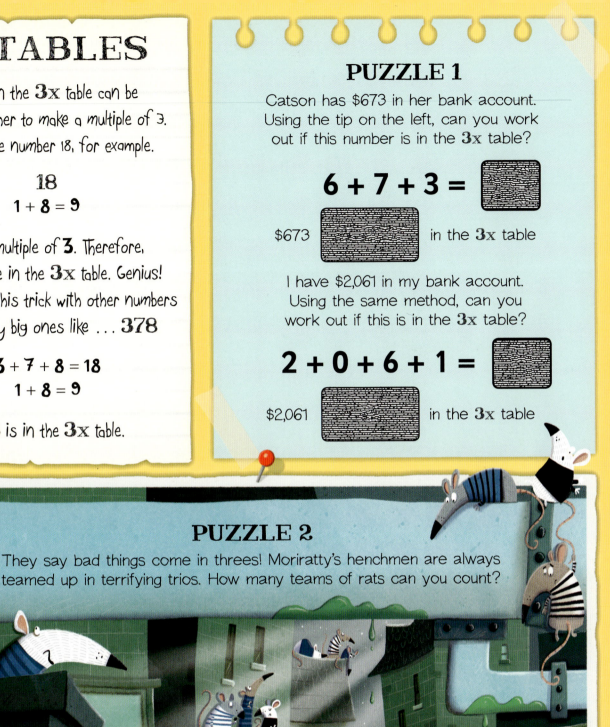

PUZZLE 2

They say bad things come in threes! Moriratty's henchmen are always teamed up in terrifying trios. How many teams of rats can you count?

Can you work out the number of rats using the **3x** table?

$$\boxed{} \; x \; 3 = \boxed{}$$

PUZZLE 3

Our police tricycles have three wheels.
There are 5 tricycles in the car park.
How many wheels are there in total?

[ ] x 3 = [ ]

PUZZLE 4

Most of the police officers in our town are pigeons and they only have three toes on each foot. Altogether, how many toes do these pigeons have?

[ ] x 3 = [ ]

QUICKFIRE QUIZ

7 x 3 = [ ]   11 x 3 = [ ]   9 x 3 = [ ]

1 x 3 = [ ]   5 x 3 = [ ]   6 x 3 = [ ]

8 x 3 = [ ]   10 x 3 = [ ]   4 x 3 = [ ]

3 x 3 = [ ]   12 x 3 = [ ]   2 x 3 = [ ]

4x TABLES

Just like the $2x$ tables, the $4x$ will ALWAYS be EVEN and end in a 0, 2, 4, 6, or 8.

If you know your $2x$ table, you can simply DOUBLE the result to calculate the $4x$ table:

$$9 \times 4 = ?$$
$$9 \times 2 = 18$$
DOUBLE 18 to make **36**
$$9 \times 4 = 36$$

PUZZLE 5

The detectives in the city are all cunning cats and dependable dogs, and they all have **four legs**. Using the $4x$ table, can you work out how many legs they have in total?

If you're unsure of the answer, try and use the **DOUBLE-UP** trick above.

[ ] x 4 = [ ]

PUZZLE 6

Catson and I need to catch a bus numbered with a multiple of 4. Can you use the $4x$ table to figure out which bus we should ride?

23   14   24   18   22   30

We should catch the [ ]

PUZZLE 7

Catson and I have found a pawprint in the center of a crime scene. It is our only lead, so we need to figure out who it belongs to. We've run the print through the database and the computer has flagged the following felons:

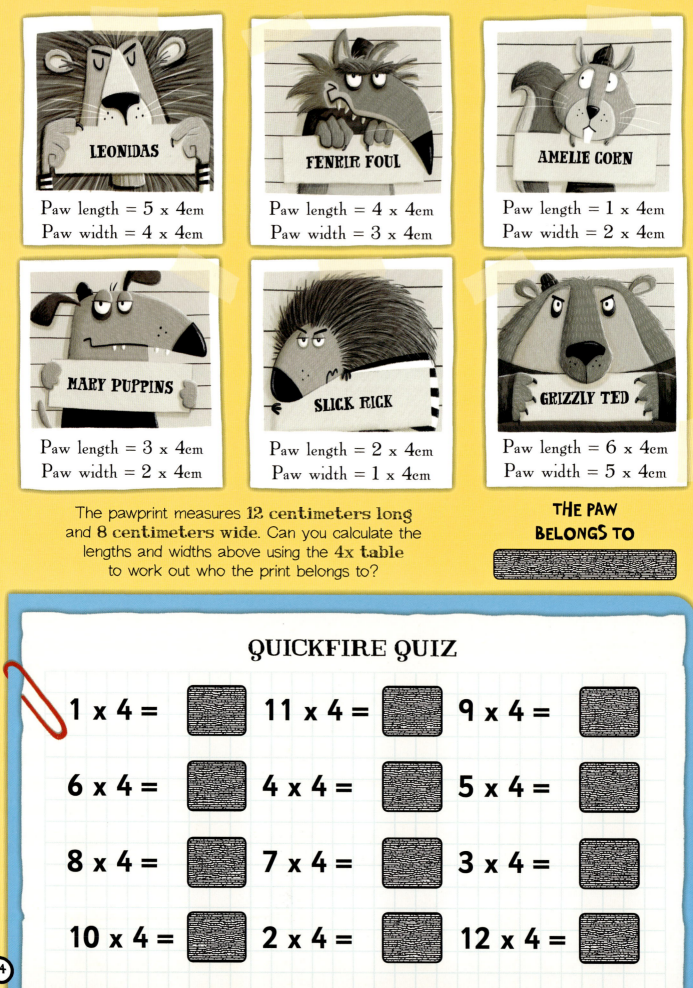

LEONIDAS

Paw length = 5 x 4cm
Paw width = 4 x 4cm

FENRIR FOUL

Paw length = 4 x 4cm
Paw width = 3 x 4cm

AMELIE CORN

Paw length = 1 x 4cm
Paw width = 2 x 4cm

MARY PUPPINS

Paw length = 3 x 4cm
Paw width = 2 x 4cm

SLICK RICK

Paw length = 2 x 4cm
Paw width = 1 x 4cm

GRIZZLY TED

Paw length = 6 x 4cm
Paw width = 5 x 4cm

The pawprint measures **12 centimeters long** and **8 centimeters wide**. Can you calculate the lengths and widths above using the **4x table** to work out who the print belongs to?

THE PAW BELONGS TO

QUICKFIRE QUIZ

1 x 4 =

11 x 4 =

9 x 4 =

6 x 4 =

4 x 4 =

5 x 4 =

8 x 4 =

7 x 4 =

3 x 4 =

10 x 4 =

2 x 4 =

12 x 4 =

8x TABLES

The **8x** table is one tough cookie to crack. There is a nifty trick to help you, though.

The column on the left is the **TENS COLUMN.** Starting at the top, the column counts **upwards** in single units, with the exception of the numbers **4 and 8**, which appear twice.

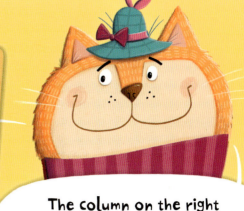

T	O
0	8
1	6
2	4
3	2
4	0
4	8
5	6
6	4
7	2
8	0
8	8
9	6

The column on the right is the **ONES COLUMN.** Starting at the top (with the number **8**), the column counts **down** in units of **2**.

Write these columns out whenever you need help with your **8x** table.

PUZZLE 8

I am terrified of spiders and always have to ask Catson to help me dispose of them. How many spiders can you spot in my study? Once you have counted them, work out how many legs there are in total. **CLUE:** Spiders have 8 legs.

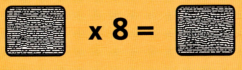

[ ] x 8 = [ ]

PUZZLE 9

After Mrs. Moo's shop got burgled, she needed to replenish her stolen stock. Her favorite number is 8, so she decided to order items in multiples of 8. Can you calculate how many items she's ordered in total?

3 x 8 apples +
4 x 8 bottles of milk +
2 x 8 chocolate bars

TOTAL =

PUZZLE 10

Dr. Octopus is a master of disguise. He sometimes helps us solve cases by going undercover and his wardrobe is full of costumes and props for his disguises.

We asked Dr. Octopus how many outfits he had. Here's his puzzling reply:

How many outfits do I have?
That's easy, the answer is 9 x 8.

ANSWER: Dr. Octopus has outfits.

QUICKFIRE QUIZ

10 x 8 =   7 x 8 =   9 x 8 =

3 x 8 =   4 x 8 =   5 x 8 =

8 x 8 =   11 x 8 =   6 x 8 =

1 x 8 =   2 x 8 =   12 x 8 =

MORIRATTY MISCHIEF
SILVER

After decoding Moriratty's note, Catson and I followed his trail to the observatory. We looked through one of the telescopes and noticed that, instead of pointing toward the stars, it pointed directly toward a group of islands in the distance. Very curious indeed! Can you follow the multiples of **3**, **4**, and **8** to show us which island Moriratty fled to? Solve the puzzle to earn your **SILVER**-level medal.

The correct island is:

GOLD: 6x, 7x, 9x TABLES

Use Sherlock's Secret Solver to see how the **GOLD** times tables work:

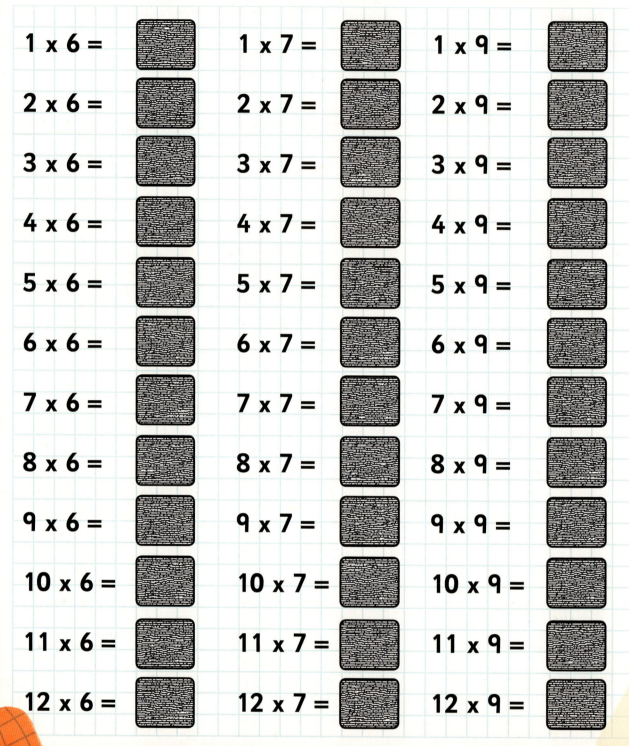

1 x 6 =

2 x 6 =

3 x 6 =

4 x 6 =

5 x 6 =

6 x 6 =

7 x 6 =

8 x 6 =

9 x 6 =

10 x 6 =

11 x 6 =

12 x 6 =

1 x 7 =

2 x 7 =

3 x 7 =

4 x 7 =

5 x 7 =

6 x 7 =

7 x 7 =

8 x 7 =

9 x 7 =

10 x 7 =

11 x 7 =

12 x 7 =

1 x 9 =

2 x 9 =

3 x 9 =

4 x 9 =

5 x 9 =

6 x 9 =

7 x 9 =

8 x 9 =

9 x 9 =

10 x 9 =

11 x 9 =

12 x 9 =

Here's my best **GOLD**-level tip:
If you're struggling with some of the multiples,
it's sometimes best to start off with multiples you
do know. Can you try and add or subtract
from them to figure out the answer?

6x TABLES

The **6x** table is one of the more difficult to learn, but can you remember the trick I taught you for the **3x** table? Well, it also works for the **6x** table. The digits in the answers can be added together to create a multiple of 3.

Take 36, for example. 3 + 6 = 9 and 9 is a multiple of 3.

If you have a really big number, you can simply keep adding the digits in the multiple together, until you're left with just one figure. If we start with **885**, for instance, we can add 8 + 8 + 5, which makes **21**. We then combine **2** and 1 to make **3**, which means **885** is a multiple of 3.

Not only will the numbers in the 6x table add up to create a multiple of 3, they also always end in the EVEN number they are multiplied by. The answer to 2×6, for example, ends in a 2. The answer to 4×6 ends in a 4, and so on . . .

PUZZLE 1

When Catson and I get a day off, we like to play board games. Catson loves playing with the dice and is always trying to roll as many sixes as she can. Counting JUST the sixes, what is her total score below? Use you **6x** tables to work out the answer.

TOTAL =

PUZZLE 2

This is Captain McCluckski, the bravest chicken in the roost. She's been trying to catch a master egg thief for some time and has finally found his hideout. The eggs are all organized into batches of half a dozen. Can you count all of the eggs using your **6x** table?

TOTAL =

PUZZLE 3

Catson and I are patrolling the sewers in search of Moriratty's gang. Before we left the station, we had to order all sorts of supplies for our **6-person** patrol. Can you work out how many of each item we had to order?

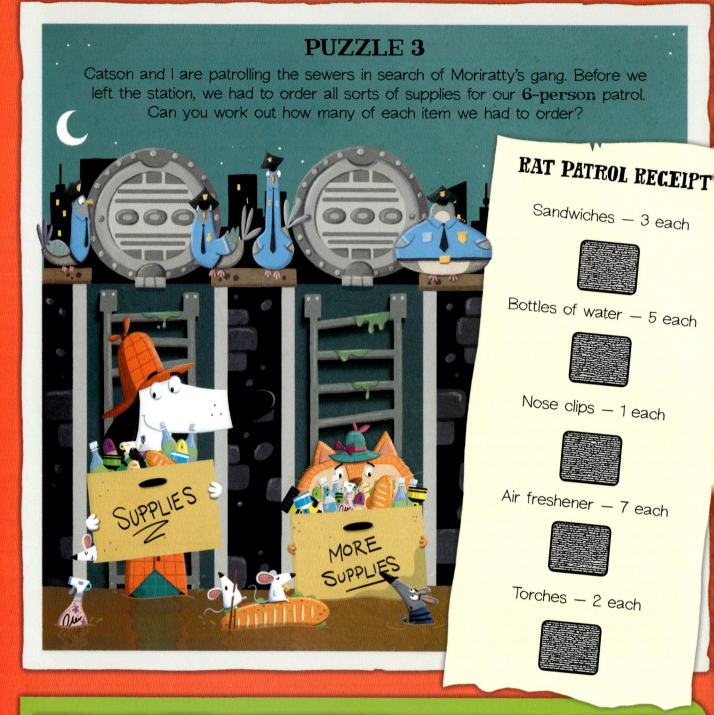

RAT PATROL RECEIPT

Sandwiches — 3 each

Bottles of water — 5 each

Nose clips — 1 each

Air freshener — 7 each

Torches — 2 each

QUICKFIRE QUIZ

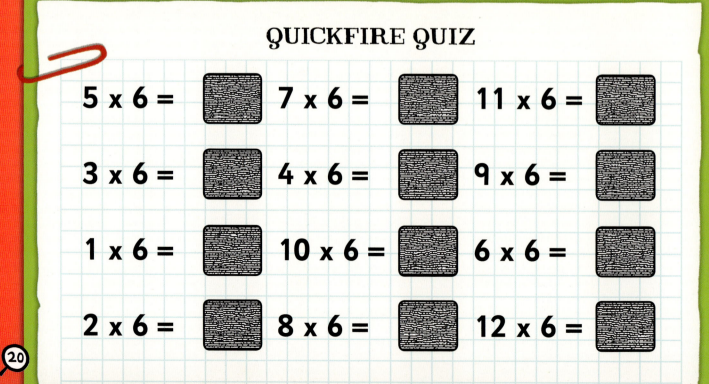

5 x 6 =

7 x 6 =

11 x 6 =

3 x 6 =

4 x 6 =

9 x 6 =

1 x 6 =

10 x 6 =

6 x 6 =

2 x 6 =

8 x 6 =

12 x 6 =

7x TABLES

One of the best ways of learning the 7x table is to use the tables that you already know by either adding to or subtracting from them to find your answer. If, for example, you're trying to work out 8 x 7, and you already know your 6x table, you can use this simple trick:

$$8 \times 7 = ?$$
$$8 \times 6 = 48$$

Then simply add 8 to 48 to make 7 sets of 8, rather than 6.
There you have it!

PUZZLE 4

Catson and I are trying to work out when to take a day trip to the countryside. We'd like to go on a Sunday. Using your 7x table, can you work out which Sunday is suitable by reading through the clues and looking at the calendar below?

← **Start** from here and move up in mutiples of seven.

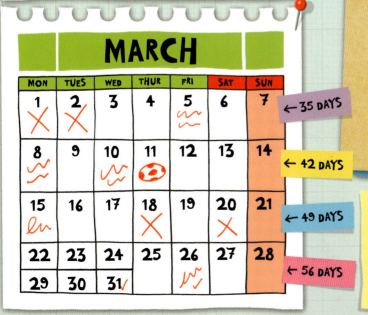

CLUES

STARTING FROM THE **O** ...

We are due in court
4 x 7 days from now

We are having lunch with
Mrs Moo in 1 x 7 days

We are getting our claws
clipped in 7 x 7 days

We are working on the weekend
2 x 7 and 3 x 7 days from now

We are going to the theatre
8 x 7 days from now

We are playing pawball
5 x 7 days from now

← 35 DAYS

← 42 DAYS

← 49 DAYS

← 56 DAYS

We can go to the countryside on

PUZZLE 5

This is **BARKER STREET**, where I live. Using your **7x** table, can you work out the missing house numbers?

QUICKFIRE QUIZ

4 x 7 =   5 x 7 =   1 x 7 =

7 x 7 =   12 x 7 =   3 x 7 =

2 x 7 =   8 x 7 =   6 x 7 =

11 x 7 =   9 x 7 =   10 x 7 =

9x TABLES

Use this nifty trick when you want help with your **9x** tables.

1) Place your hands (or paws) flat against the table.

2) Counting from the left, bend the finger you are multiplying by. In this case, I'm multiplying 4 x 9, so I bend the fourth finger from the left.

3) Count the fingers that remain. The fingers to the left-hand side of the bent finger are the tens. The fingers to the right are the ones. In this case we can count three tens and six ones, making 36.

PUZZLE 6

The cats in our town have 9 lives. It's a useful trait to have when catching master criminals. Can you count the cats in this scene and use your **9x** table to work out how many lives they have in total?

Number of lives:

PUZZLE 7

Mr. Spriggs works at the Piggy Bank. Some crafty robbers tried to break in last night and Mr. Spriggs wants to open some of the vaults to check that nothing has been stolen. Can you use your **9x** table to work out whether any money is missing?

VAULT 1

VAULT 2

VAULT 3

SHOULD HAVE $72
HAS $8 X 9

THIS VAULT

BEEN BURGLED

SHOULD HAVE $108
HAS $12 X 9

THIS VAULT

BEEN BURGLED

SHOULD HAVE $999
HAS $1 X 9

THIS VAULT

BEEN BURGLED

QUICKFIRE QUIZ

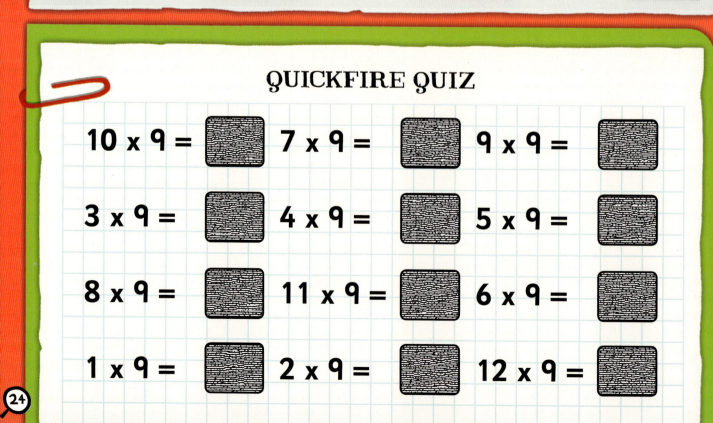

10 x 9 =

7 x 9 =

9 x 9 =

3 x 9 =

4 x 9 =

5 x 9 =

8 x 9 =

11 x 9 =

6 x 9 =

1 x 9 =

2 x 9 =

12 x 9 =

MORIRATTY MISCHIEF
GOLD

Now that we know which island Moriratty fled to, Catson and I need to find out which boat he chartered so that we end up on the right part of the island. Catson searched the jetty and found Moriratty's discarded ticket stub. Can you match the numbers on the ticket to its corresponding ship? Solve the puzzle to earn your **GOLD**-level medal.

CHARTERED SHIPS

PORTSIDE HARBOR

No: 42 81 63
14 84 108

THE LEVIATHAN

7 x 6   8 x 9   7 x 9
2 x 7   12 x 7   12 x 9

Destination: **THE CROOKED COVE**

THE VORTEX

7 x 6   9 x 9   7 x 9
2 x 7   11 x 7   12 x 9

Destination: **THE WICKED WHIRLPOOL**

THE DOLPHIN

6 x 6   9 x 9   7 x 9
2 x 7   12 x 7   12 x 9

Destination: **THE DUNES OF DOOM**

THE KRAKEN

7 x 6   9 x 9   5 x 9
2 x 7   12 x 7   12 x 9

Destination: **THE PLANES OF PERIL**

THE DAMSEL

7 x 6   9 x 9   7 x 9
2 x 7   12 x 7   12 x 9

Destination: **THE CRAMPED CAVES**

THE DAMP SQUIB

7 x 6   9 x 9   5 x 9
2 x 7   12 x 7   12 x 9

Destination:
THE ROCKY RUINS

The correct ship is:

PLATINUM: 11x, 12x TABLES

Use Sherlock's Secret Solver to see how the **PLATINUM** times tables work:

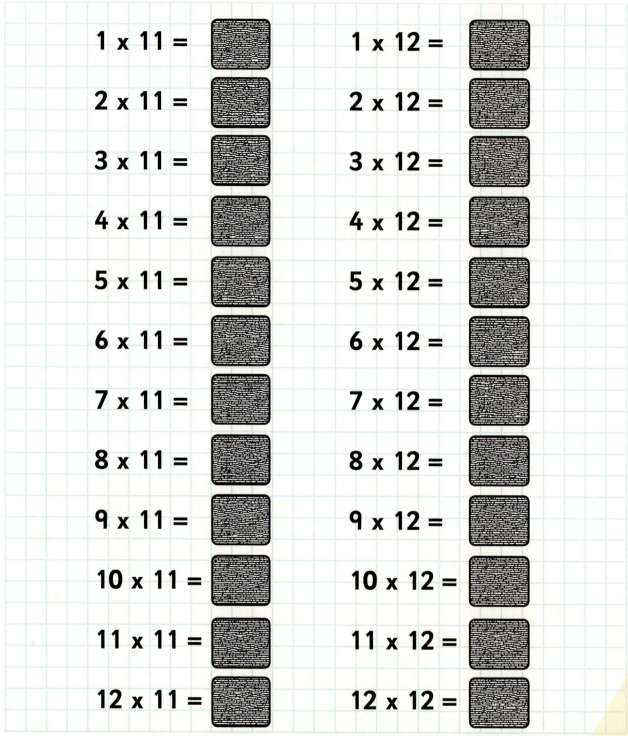

1 x 11 =

1 x 12 =

2 x 11 =

2 x 12 =

3 x 11 =

3 x 12 =

4 x 11 =

4 x 12 =

5 x 11 =

5 x 12 =

6 x 11 =

6 x 12 =

7 x 11 =

7 x 12 =

8 x 11 =

8 x 12 =

9 x 11 =

9 x 12 =

10 x 11 =

10 x 12 =

11 x 11 =

11 x 12 =

12 x 11 =

12 x 12 =

Before you begin, here's Catson's best **PLATINUM**-level tip:

Whoa! These puzzles are mind-boggling!
If you're finding these tough, you could always try
and break the times tables down into smaller chunks.
Take 7 x 11, for example. If you can't calculate the
answer in one go, you could try 7 x 10 + 7 x 1.
For 12 x 12, you could add 10 x 12 and 2 x 12.

11x TABLES

The **11x** table follows an extremely simple pattern until you reach the tenth multiple. To help you earn your **PLATINUM** badge, it's useful to remember that a number in the **11x** table will always end in the last digit of the number it's multiplied by. So, for instance:

12 x 11 will end in a 2

8 x 11 will end in an 8

164 x 11 will end in a 4

. . . and so on . . .

PUZZLE 1

When Catson and I have a break, we like to play darts at the police station. Today, we are only allowed to hit the number 11. Can you work out the scores by looking at the dart boards below? Catson's darts are red and mine are blue.

This is the DOUBLES band. The score of a dart in this space must be multiplied by 2.

This is the TRIPLES band. The score of a dart in this space must be multiplied by 3.

ROUND 1

SCORE: ROUND 1

SHERLOCK	CATSON

ROUND 2

SCORE: ROUND 2

SHERLOCK	CATSON

PUZZLE 2

Catson and I are in an amateur pawball league. We play for the **BLIGHTY BONE RANGERS** and are currently second in the league table. Can you use the 11x table to answer the questions below?

DIDIER DOGBA

PREMIER PAWBALL LEAGUE

POSITION	TEAM	POINTS
1	GRIMSBY REAPERS	33
2	BLIGHTY BONE RANGERS	26
3	UNTIDY UNITED	23
4	FIERCE CATS F.C.	22
5	CRYSTAL FALLACY	19
6	GRAVY BOYS	18
7	ABCDE F.C.	15
8	FARCELONA F.C.	11
9	ROCK BOTTOMS	9
10	BATH DODGERS	7

There are 11 players in each team. How many players are there in the whole league?

Which teams have a points total that is a multiple of 11?

A win is worth three points and the Grimsby Reapers have won every game so far. How many games have they played?

QUICKFIRE QUIZ

10 x 11 =

7 x 11 =

9 x 11 =

3 x 11 =

4 x 11 =

5 x 11 =

8 x 11 =

11 x 11 =

6 x 11 =

1 x 11 =

2 x 11 =

12 x 11 =

12x TABLES

You can use a quick trick to fast-track your learning of the **12x** table! Take a look at these two columns of numbers.

Starting at the top, the **TENS COLUMN** on the left counts **upward** in single units. Make sure you skip 5 and 11, though.

T	O
0	0
1	2
2	4
3	6
4	8
6	0
7	2
8	4
9	6
10	8
12	0
13	2
14	4

Starting at the top, the **ONES COLUMN** on the right counts **up** in units of **2**.

Write these columns on a scrap of paper whenever you find the **12x** table difficult.

PUZZLE 3

Catson and I need to offer a medal to the detective who successfully solved the biggest percentage of their cases this year. Using your **12x** table, can you work out which detective should win the award? You will need to subtract the number of unsolved cases from the total.

SPARK PUG

Solved cases:
12 x 12

Unsolved cases:
7 x 12

CINDY CLAWFORD

Solved cases:
11 x 12

Unsolved cases:
6 x 12

DROOLIUS CAESAR

Solved cases:
8 x 12

Unsolved cases:
2 x 12

The medal should go to

PUZZLE 4

We have 12 citizens on the jury in the **CREATURE COURT**.
Can you solve the questions below using your 12x table?

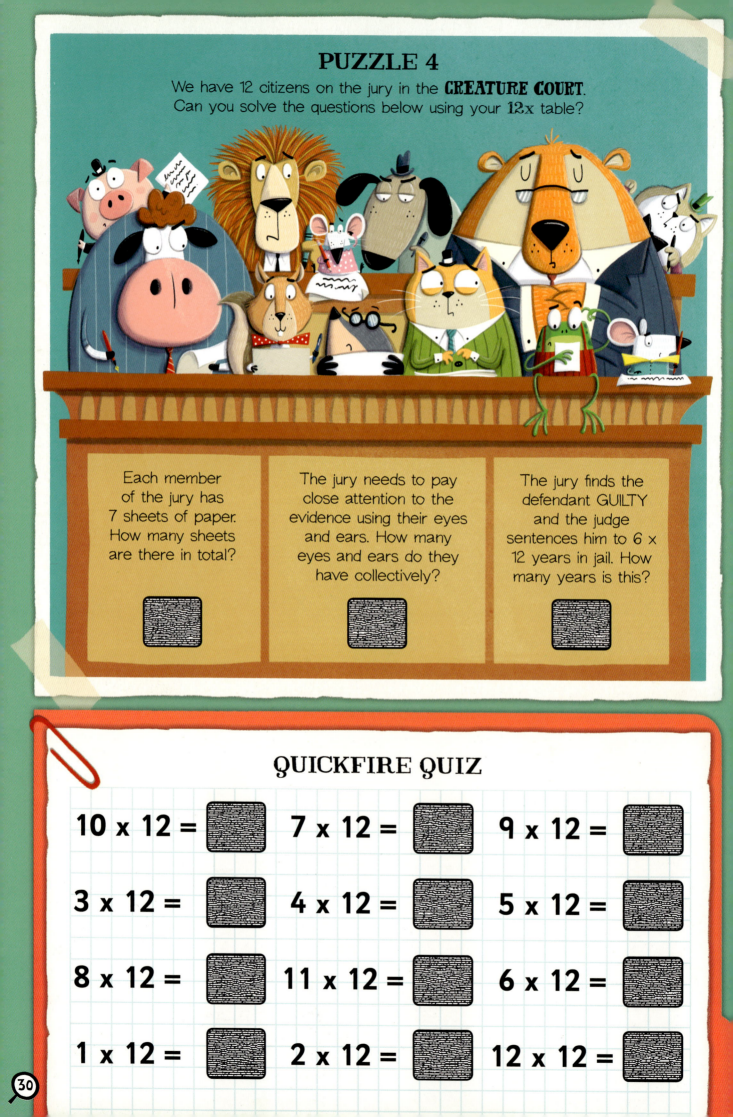

Each member of the jury has 7 sheets of paper. How many sheets are there in total?

The jury needs to pay close attention to the evidence using their eyes and ears. How many eyes and ears do they have collectively?

The jury finds the defendant GUILTY and the judge sentences him to 6 x 12 years in jail. How many years is this?

QUICKFIRE QUIZ

10 x 12 =

7 x 12 =

9 x 12 =

3 x 12 =

4 x 12 =

5 x 12 =

8 x 12 =

11 x 12 =

6 x 12 =

1 x 12 =

2 x 12 =

12 x 12 =

MORIRATTY MISCHIEF PLATINUM

Catson and I made it to the Cramped Caves and we now need to find Moriratty's evil lair. Can you guide us in the right direction by following the multiplication-themed puzzles to earn your **PLATINUM**-level medal? Your route should only follow the answers you believe to be correct.

The Cramped Caves are full of precious stones. If 12 miners find 11 stones each, how many have they found in total?

132

11 busy bats are hunting in this chamber. They each catch 7 insects. How many insects have they caught in total?

77

86

121

It is very dark in here, so Catson and I are counting our steps. So far, we've taken 8 x 12 steps. How many steps have we traveled in total?

Look at all that gold! There are 8 piles of gold in this cave. Each pile has 11 nuggets. How many nuggets are there in total?

OH NO! We've fallen into the Pit of Peril! Go back to the beginning and try your times tables again.

102

96

88

81

72

12 rats are scurrying in the darkness. How many eyes and legs do they have in total?

We've hit a dead end. Go back to the beginning and find a way through the caves.

Catson and I have now taken 12 x 12 steps. How many steps have we traveled?

68

Oh no! This path is blocked by rubble. Go back the other way.

142

Wrong turn! Go back to the previous step.

144

MIXED MADNESS
MORIRATTY MISCHIEF

We've got Professor Moriratty cornered. Catson and I need to cross the **Grid of Terror** in order to arrest him. Can you find the correct path by solving the times tables?

To earn your **DETECTIVE** badge and prove that you truly are terrific at times tables, simply multiply the number in the red box along the top row by the corresponding number down the left-hand column. Follow the path to reap your reward.

	1	2	3	4	5	6	7	8	9	10	11	12
1			3	4				8	9	10	11	12
2	2			8		12		16	18			
3	3	6				18		24			33	
4	4	8	12	16	20	24					40	44
5	5	10				30	35	40	45	50	55	
6	6	12		24								
7	7			28	35	42	49	56	63	70	77	84
8	8		24	32					72			
9	9		27	36		54	63		81		99	
10	10		30	40		60			90		110	
11	11					66		88	99		121	
12	12	24	36	48	60	72					132	

This is to certify that you are a
TIMES TABLE MASTER
Sherlock Bones